Mitko Bogdanoski
Aleksandar Risteski
Marjan Bogdanoski

Cyber operations - a permanent part of the global conflict

AF153519

Mitko Bogdanoski
Aleksandar Risteski
Marjan Bogdanoski

Cyber operations - a permanent part of the global conflict

LAP LAMBERT Academic Publishing

Impressum / Imprint

Bibliografische Information der Deutschen Nationalbibliothek: Die Deutsche Nationalbibliothek verzeichnet diese Publikation in der Deutschen Nationalbibliografie; detaillierte bibliografische Daten sind im Internet über http://dnb.d-nb.de abrufbar.
Alle in diesem Buch genannten Marken und Produktnamen unterliegen warenzeichen-, marken- oder patentrechtlichem Schutz bzw. sind Warenzeichen oder eingetragene Warenzeichen der jeweiligen Inhaber. Die Wiedergabe von Marken, Produktnamen, Gebrauchsnamen, Handelsnamen, Warenbezeichnungen u.s.w. in diesem Werk berechtigt auch ohne besondere Kennzeichnung nicht zu der Annahme, dass solche Namen im Sinne der Warenzeichen- und Markenschutzgesetzgebung als frei zu betrachten wären und daher von jedermann benutzt werden dürften.

Bibliographic information published by the Deutsche Nationalbibliothek: The Deutsche Nationalbibliothek lists this publication in the Deutsche Nationalbibliografie; detailed bibliographic data are available in the Internet at http://dnb.d-nb.de.
Any brand names and product names mentioned in this book are subject to trademark, brand or patent protection and are trademarks or registered trademarks of their respective holders. The use of brand names, product names, common names, trade names, product descriptions etc. even without a particular marking in this works is in no way to be construed to mean that such names may be regarded as unrestricted in respect of trademark and brand protection legislation and could thus be used by anyone.

Coverbild / Cover image: www.ingimage.com

Verlag / Publisher:
LAP LAMBERT Academic Publishing
ist ein Imprint der / is a trademark of
OmniScriptum GmbH & Co. KG
Heinrich-Böcking-Str. 6-8, 66121 Saarbrücken, Deutschland / Germany
Email: info@lap-publishing.com

Herstellung: siehe letzte Seite /
Printed at: see last page
ISBN: 978-3-659-52016-7

CONTENTS

LIST OF FIGURES

LIST OF TABLES

1. INTRODUCTION

The existence of a modern society nowadays is almost inconceivable without having to follow the latest technological achievements. The dependence of the individuals and society on computer systems, communications, robotics, drones and other advance technology, becomes greater. To take full advantage of the capabilities of modern technology it is necessary to be connected with the outside world through a global network, because otherwise the investments in the rapid technological development would be unacceptable for the simple reason that one of the basic needs of all (whether they are individuals, groups, industrialists, government officials, etc.) is to be always and everywhere connected and up to date. People, machines, businesses, organizations and even things have ever increasing need for communication in everyday life.

Global and seamless connectivity today is enabled by complex telecommunication infrastructure consisted of a large variety of different technologies which are in continuous process of development and innovations. Cheap and easy access to the globally connected world (provided by new devices, applications, services ...) are the reason for increased number of users which operates on everyday Internet usage. In the last years there is huge expansion in the usage of telecommunication infrastructure. Moreover, the ICT is one of the key drivers for general growth.

In order to make this possible, the researchers are working on improvement on the existing technologies, which allows increased Internet speed, increased mobility, increased security etc.

However, besides the positive effects, the global connectivity and easy access to the modern technologies also enables malicious users in their activities. They can access in the systems and networks without authorization, and moreover the global network offers them an opportunity to bind together across the globe, thus increasing their capacities and capabilities. In the last period, there are many examples of cyber attacks where the effects turns from passive into destructive, which includes disabling the normal operation of the ICT infrastructure or even destroying data and systems, attacks on critical infrastructure, entire nations, even global society.

Due to the increased number of cyber attacks, where the attackers are taking advantage over non secured computer systems and networks can cause complete blockade of the functionality of the nation's critical information infrastructure, the protection of information and communication system has become one of the major global security concerns.

Cyber attacks are treated as the most dangerous in the case when they are used by terrorist organizations to realize their goals. The use of so called cyber weapons by the terrorists in achieving their goals is often called cyber terrorism.

Although there are a number of definitions which describe the term terrorism, one of the definitions that are frequently encountered is that terrorism is "the unlawful use or threatening use of force or violence by a person or an organized group against people or property with the intention of intimidating or forcing societies or governments, often for ideological or political reasons."[1]

Interactions between human motives and information technology for terrorist activities in cyberspace or in the virtual world can be addressed as cyber terrorism. Yet this is the definition of cyber terrorism that Sarah Gordon and Richard Ford from Symantec have used in their efforts to define "pure Cyberterrorism." [2]

The cyber terrorism as a concept has various definitions, mostly because every expert in security has its own definition. This term can be defined as the use of information technology by terrorist groups or individuals to achieve their goals. This may include the use of information technology to organize and execute attacks against networks, computer systems and telecommunications infrastructure, and to exchange information and perform electronic threat. This kind of security threat can manifest itself in many ways, such as hacking computer systems, programming viruses and worms, Web pages attack, conducting denial of service (DoS) attacks, or conducting terrorist attacks through electronic communications. More common are claims that cyber terrorism does not exist and that actually it is a hacking and malicious attacks. Those who support these claims do not agree with the term "terrorism" because if we take into account the current technologies for prevention and care, the likelihood of creating fear, significant physical damage or death among population using electronic means would be very small.

Considering the fact that the terrorists have limited funds, cyber attacks are increasingly attractive, because, their implementation requires a smaller number of people and certainly smaller funds. Another advantage of cyber attacks is that they allow terrorists to remain unknown, because they can be very far from the place where the act of terrorism is committed. Unlike the terrorists that place their camps in countries with weak governance, cyber terrorists can store anywhere and remain anonymous. [3] It is believed that the most effective use of cyber terrorism is when it is used in combination with physical terrorism. For example, disabling the operation of emergency services in situations where the need for deployment of such services is caused by the use of physical terrorism is really an effective way of pooling of mentioned types of terrorism. There are huge possibilities of conducting cyber terrorism through Internet using advanced technology. As possible targets of cyber terrorism can be considered government computer networks, financial networks, power plants, etc., and the reason for this is that the terrorists identifies all the above as most suitable targets to be damaged or put out of operation in order to cause chaos. Systems manipulation through "secret entrance" software, stealing classified information, data deletion, Web sites damaging, viruses inserting, etc. are just a few examples of how terrorists can enter into the secured system. The terrorist attacks enabled by computer technology can be also conducted through the air traffic control system or by remote damage of the power supply networks.

The new information technologies (IT) and the Internet are more often used by terrorist organizations in conducting of their plans to raise the financial funds, distribute their propaganda and secure communications. Director of the Central Intelligence Agency (CIA), George Tenet, in his statement in 2000 for global security threats, explained that the terrorist groups including Hezbollah's, Hamas and al-Qaeda, for support of their operations, use computerized files, e-mails and protection (encryption). The convicted terrorist Ramzi Yousef, the main planner of the attack on the World Trade Centre in New York in encrypted files in his laptop computer stored detailed plans for aircraft destruction in the United States. [4]

The terrorist organizations also use the Internet to "reach out" their

4

audience, without need to use other media such as radio, television or holding various press conferences. Web pages are used as a way to highlight injustice and to seek support for as the call "political prisoners" which are "illegally captured". Typical Web pages will not display any information related to the violent activities and will usually claim to be left with no other choice but to resort to violence. They claim to be persecuted, that their leaders have been targets of assassination and their supporters were massacred. They use this tactic to give impression that they are weak and to present themselves as outsiders. This public performance is a very easy way to recruit supporters and members. Besides propaganda, on the terrorist organizations Web sites can often be found content and instructions on how to make explosives and chemical weapons. This allows them to identify the most common users that can have sympathy for their cause and because of that this is an effective method for recruiting.

This also helps individuals acting as terrorists to engage in terrorist activities. In 1999, a terrorist named David Copeland killed 3 people and injured 139 in London. He did this with the help of bombs placed in three different locations. At his trial it was discovered that he used Terrorists Manual (Terrorist Handbook - Forest, 2005) and How to Make a Bomb (How to Make Bombs - Bombs, 2004), which had downloaded from the Internet. [5]

The rest of the book is organized as follows. Chapter 2 gives an overview of the treatment of cyber attacks by the world's superpowers, as well as large security related organizations. Chapter 3 covers the most modern and most destructive cyber attacks which can disrupt the global security, including the most resent concepts of cyber warfare. Cyber terrorism and method and techniques of cyber terrorism are described in Chapter 4. Brief description of the national responses to the threats of cyber terrorism is given in Chapter 5. Furthermore, Chapter 6 gives a description of the multinational responses to the treats of cyber terrorism. Chapter 7 gives explanation about possible implementation of the International humanitarian law in the case of cyber operations (cyber attack or cyber terrorism). Finally, Chapter 7 concludes our work.

2. THE PLACE OF THE CYBER ATTACKS AMONG THE GLOBAL SECURITY THREATS

In the last years, malwares, Trojans, vulnerabilities of computer systems, networks' vulnerabilities, intrusions, data theft, identity theft, botnets and critical infrastructure protection are becoming common major issue on conferences and other events related to the security threats.

Many public discussions are focused on threats and methods in order to develop better defence mechanisms. On the other hand, the governments do not want to talk neither about the methods of cyber attacks and operations nor the followed policy during the cyber operations. The reason for this concealment is perhaps the fear that people will not approve these operations.

Due to the increased usage of cyberspace to attack not just a computer system or a critical infrastructure, but the entire nation's functionality, the world's superpowers and large organizations take appropriate and timely measures and strive to follow the progress of a growing army of malicious users.

Thinking in this direction resulted mostly after the cyber attacks against Estonia in 2007 followed by similar attacks in several other countries, where "army" of attacker's and zombie's machines completely blocked functionality of several critical institutions in this country.

One of the main countermeasures taken by USA in 2010 against the increased number and power of the malicious users was establishment of a new Cyber Command (also known as USCYBERCOM) whose main objectives are to coordinate cyber defence of military networks and conduct full spectrum military cyberspace operations in order to enable actions in all domains.

Similar commands/institutions are established or under establishment by the other superpowers and organizations. The investments in this field are more than acceptable if it is considered the place that cyber attacks takes among the global security threats [6,7,8,9,10,11] and financial losses caused by these attacks [12,13]. According to security concepts, strategies and other documents adopted by the biggest security related organizations as well as nations' strategies and policies [14,15,16,17], these attacks again take place among the highest security threats.

In June 2011, then-CIA (Central Intelligence Agency) Director Leon Panetta stated that "The next Pearl Harbor we confront could very well be a cyber-attack that cripples our government, security and financial systems" [17]. Later, he also gave an interview for CBC News [18], but now as a Secretary of Defence, where he showed concerns from these attacks and the possible consequences. Paneta said that "cyber warfare can threaten the grid system, the financial system, and even it could paralyze whole nation".[19]

On the other hand, FBI (Federal Bureau of Investigation) since 2009 ranked cyber attacks as the third most dangerous threats behind nuclear war and weapons of mass destruction [20].

Table 1. Most known cyber attacks on national/global security and critical infrastructure

Year	Attacker	Target	Consequences
1982	USA-CIA	Logic bomb targeting USSR Siberian gas pipeline	Destruction
1999 and 2000	Russia	Pentagon, NASA, National Labs	Stealing information, espionage
2004	China	Sandia National Laboratory, Lockheed Martin and NASA	Espionage
2007	China	U.S. Computer Network (750,000 computers)	Denial of service
2007	Русија	Estonia's government websites and other important institutions/banks	Denial of service
2008	Unknown	U.S. Military Network	Malicious code and zombie machines
2008	China and/or Russia	U.S. Presidential Election	Intrusion into email systems
2008	Russia	Georgia's government websites and other important institutions/banks	Denial of service
2010, 2011	Unknown (unofficial Israel/USA)	Iranian uranium enrichment centrifuges	Sabotage
2010-2013	Anonymous "Operation Avenge Assange"	Multiple western targets (public and private)	Denial of service
April 2011	2 anonymous groups/ supported by unknown state	RSA Secure ID	Phishing, Espionage
August 2012	Unknown (unofficial Iran) Cutting Sword of Justice	Saudi Aramco oil company	Destruction, Espionage

2013	USA - NSA	United Nation's video conferencing system European Union building on New York International Atomic Energy Agency	Surveillance

Table 1 shows the most known cyber attacks targeting important state's public and private institutions. The most of the cyber attacks are largely limited to denial of service, espionage and sabotage [21].

Among the attacks shown in Table 1 we would emphasize the attack on U.S. military network in 2008. The Pentagon had never openly discussed the incident. According to the statement given in 2009 by the Deputy Secretary of Defence, William Lynn, this attack is treated as the most serious attack on classified U.S. military networks. It began when an infected flash drive was inserted into a U.S. military laptop at a base in the Middle East. The flash drive's malicious computer code, placed there by a foreign intelligence agency, uploaded itself onto a network run by the U.S. Central Command. That code spread undetected on both classified and unclassified systems, establishing what amounted to a digital beachhead, from which data could be transferred to servers under foreign control. It was a network administrator's worst fear: a rogue program operating silently, poised to deliver operational plans into the hands of an unknown adversary [22].

Stuxnet and especially Duqu, targeting the Iranian uranium enrichment centrifuges, are operating on very similar way with this malicious code, especially considering the way of spreading among the networks and systems and sending the steeled information back to the attacker [23].

The telecommunication providers and infrastructure are not resistant to these attacks. There are many examples for malicious activities against this infrastructure.

One of the latest examples of cyber attacks on telecommunication infrastructure was the advance massive cyber attack on Telenor, the telecommunication giant of Norway [24]. It's perceived that cyber-criminals may have filched significant volume of information stored on computers that the executives of the major organization used. To be able to enter in the provider's infrastructure the attackers initially attacked dispatched crafty emails that hit the inboxes of the high-profile officials, while seemed as arriving from trustworthy sources as internal employees and organization. There were attachments too inside the e-mails whose files carried advanced malicious software undetectable by security software.

Even more, in December 2012, during the World Conference on International Telecommunications (WCIT) held in Dubai, hackers disabled the ITU's (International Telecommunication Agency) main meeting and several websites [25].

3. THE MOST RESENT CONCEPTS OF THE CYBER ATTACKS

Although cyber security came into use in the ICT sector since the first computer systems, it was only in 2007, when large-scale cyber attacks came over entire nation, that the topic was catapulted to the centre of international attention. This was a warning to all world's superpowers for a new type of threat that for a short time will become one of the greatest threats to the global security [26].

For better understanding of this global security threat the section firstly will describe the most common attacks that fall into this group of threats. In the list that follows, the attacks are listed according to their impact, from the simplest to the most destructive [23].

- **Cyber espionage**

  Cyber espionage is the act or practice of obtaining secrets (sensitive, private or classified information) from individuals, competitors, rivals, enemies and governments for military, political or economic advantage using illegal methods for exploitation of internet, networks, software and / or computers.

- **WEB vandalism**

  These are attacks that defacement of the websites or denial of service attacks.

- **Propaganda**

  In this kind of attack it is possible to send political messages to anyone who has access to the Internet.

- **Information gathering**

  This attack is used to intercept or modify the information, making espionage possible from any part of the world.

- **Distributed denial of service attack**

  It is a type of DOS attack where multiple compromised system, which are usually infected with a Trojan, are used to target a single system causing a Denial of Service (DoS) attack. Victims of a DDoS (Distributed DoS) attack consist of both the end targeted system and all systems maliciously used and controlled by the hacker in the distributed attack.

- **Equipment disruption**

  Victims of this attack are military operations that are used to coordinate computers and satellites. Using this attack, malicious users can intercept or modify orders and communications, putting soldiers at risk.

- **Attacking critical infrastructure**

  Using this attack, the malicious user can penetrate the control systems of the electricity, water, fuel, communications, transportation and similar key infrastructure elements and provide control over them.

- **Compromised counterfeit hardware**

  This attack refers to common hardware used in computers and networks that have malware hidden inside software, firmware or even in microprocessors.

Always at the end of the year, the experts and organizations that deal with computer security are trying to make predictions about the possible threats for next year. Many of the threats that become prominent in the following year are already been looming discernible under the radar in the current year.

According to [27,28,29], the top cyber threats predictions for 2013 are:

- Criminals will benefit from unintended consequences of espionage,
- Attackers will increasingly use apps, movies and music to install malware,
- Drive-by attacks and cross-site scripting attacks will be attacker favorites,
- Software updating gets easier and exploiting vulnerabilities gets harder,

- An increase in large-scale attacks, designed to destroy infrastructure rather than based on purely financial gain, will firmly take hold in 2013,
- Hacking "as a service" is expected to rise,
- Rootkits will evolve in 2013,
- Cyber attacks will be directed to cloud servers and mobile devices,
- The decline of Anonymous, but a rise in extreme hacktivism.

The analysis of these five predictions associated with cyber threats gives a bleak picture about the cyber attacks in 2013. Threats seem extremely challenging, if not a bit overwhelming. The sight is a modernization of the armed conflict and at this point there are more questions than answers.

The most recent analysis for cyber attacks made by Hackmageddon for August 2013, shows that US, India and UK collected together 54% of the attacks reported in the timelines (Figure 1) [30].

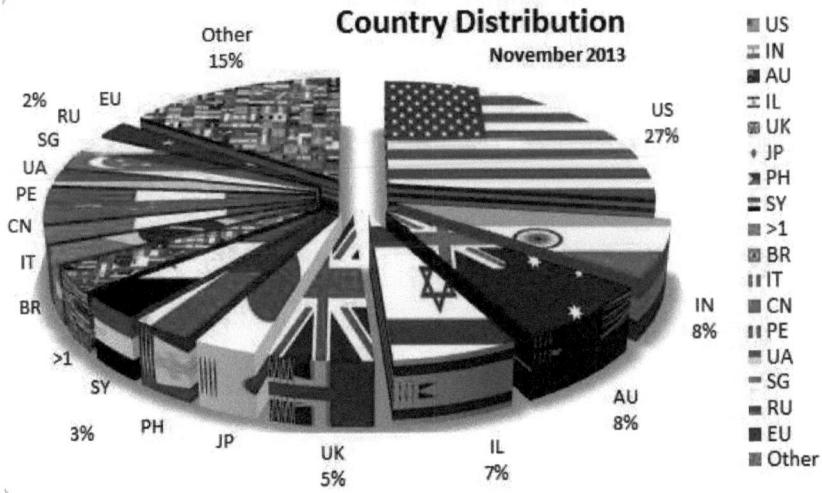

Figure 1. Cyber attack country distribution for November 2013

The same source gives a statistic showing that cyber crime is leading motivation behind cyber attack with 53% followed by hactivism.

For a long time SQLi (Structured Query Language Injection) and DDoS are among first tree ranks cyber attack [31], although in the last period Defacements lead the **Distribution of Attack Techniques** Chart (Figure 2). Also the account Hijackings are becoming very popular.

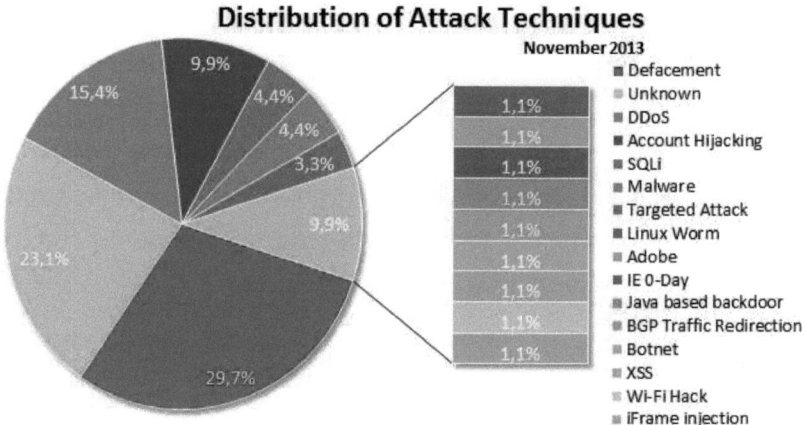

Figure 2. Distribution of attack techniques for November 2013

Apparently it is getting harder and harder to track the real technique used to carry on the attacks. According to the statistics, the reasons and mechanisms used for almost one of four attacks are unknown. However, DDoS, as usual, leads the **Distribution of Attack Techniques** chart for the known cases (Figure 2). The Syrian Electronic Army traced the line, so the influence of Account Hijacking is becoming more and more evident month after month. Instead the fall of SQLi (Structured Query Language Injection) keeps on. Apparently this technique is constantly loosing points, but it is a question how many of the "unknowns" were effectively related to SQLi.

Governmental and Industry targets lead the **Distribution of Target** chart with 26% and 17% respectively (Figure 3). These two categories are swapping their places for a long period. Very interesting point is the third position of single individuals, which are essentially victims of account hijackings.

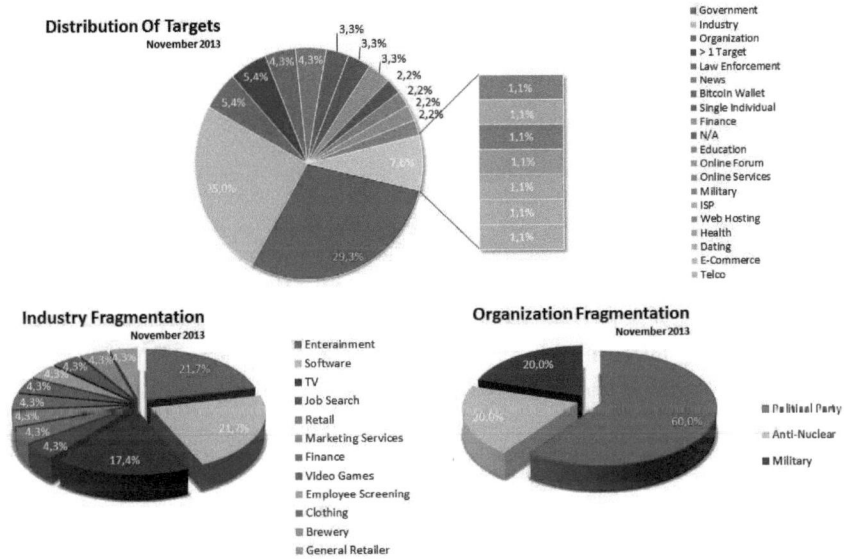

Figure 3. Distribution of targets for November 2013

Over the past years, there has been a rapid increase in the proliferation of new cyber weapons that are being used as part of coordinated cyber attacks on computer networks around the world. In some cases, these cyber attacks are part of sustained, multi-year operations that target governments, corporations and research institutions.

The most dangerous cyber weapons of 2013 with the greatest potential to change how we think about the relationship between national security and cyber security are briefly described in the following sub-sections.

3.1. Red October

At the very beginning of 2013, Kaspersky Lab published a comprehensive report that included the results of a study of the global cyber espionage operation known as "Red October". The earliest evidence indicates that cyber espionage campaign was active since 2007. The attackers have been focused on diplomatic and governmental agencies of various countries across the world. The information harvested from infected networks was reused in later attacks.[32]

Figure 4 shows country distribution of connections to the sinkhole, where it can be seen that Macedonian, as well as other countries from the region (Greece, Bulgaria, Croatia and Serbia) are represent in very large percentage. Namely, nearly one-third of the espionage attacks occurs in countries from this region.

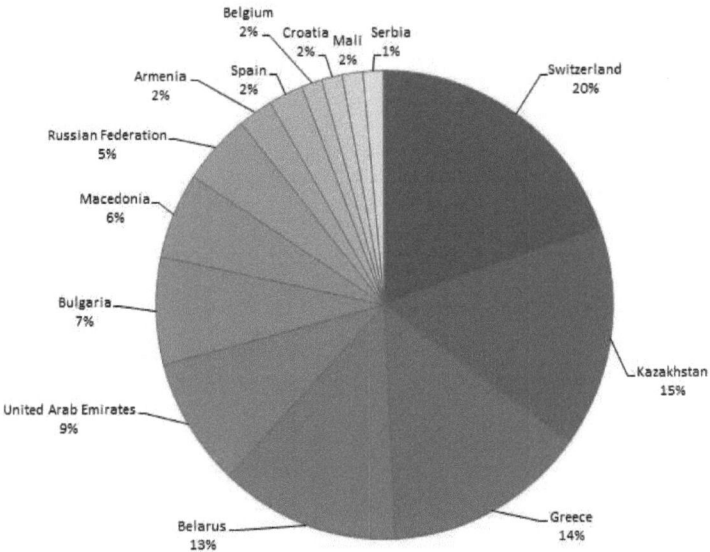

Figure 4. Red October operation - country distribution of connections to the sinkhole

3.2. MiniDuke

In February 2013, Kaspersky Labs identifies 'MiniDuke', a new malicious program designed for spying on multiple government entities and institutions across the world (Figure 5). Cyber criminals have targeted government officials in more than 20 countries, including Ireland and Romania, in a complex online assault seen rarely since the turn of the millennium. The attack was conducted using Adobe PDF bug. [33]

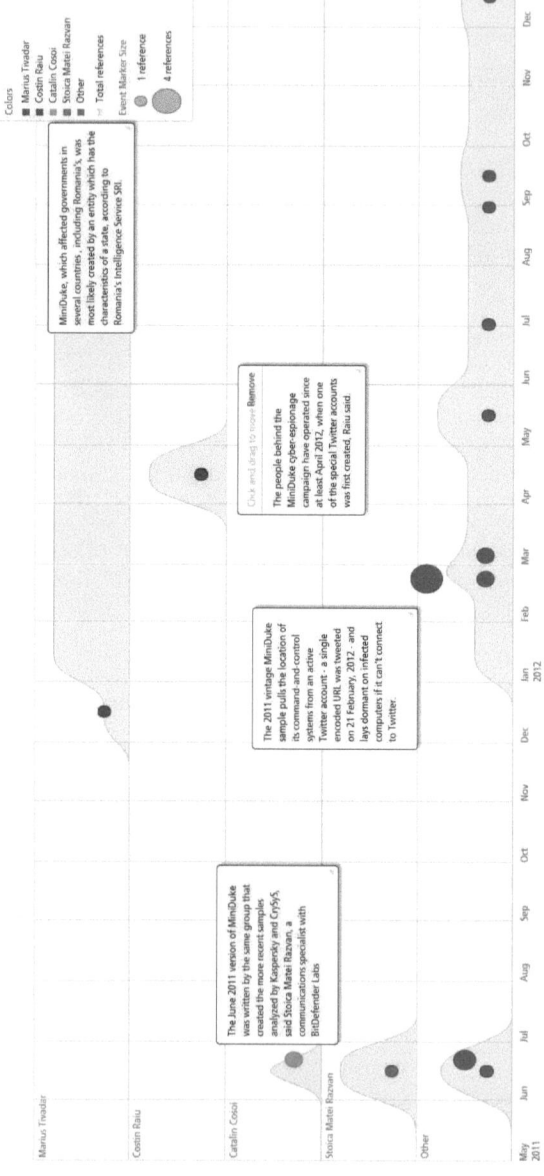

MiniDuke History

Figure 5. MiniDuke History

18

3.3. APT1 (Advanced Persistent Threat)

In February 2013 U.S. information security company Mandiant published a comprehensive report on attacks by a group of Chinese hackers known as APT1 (Figure 6). At the beginning of the report, Mandiant states that APT1 is believed to be a unit of the Chinese Army.

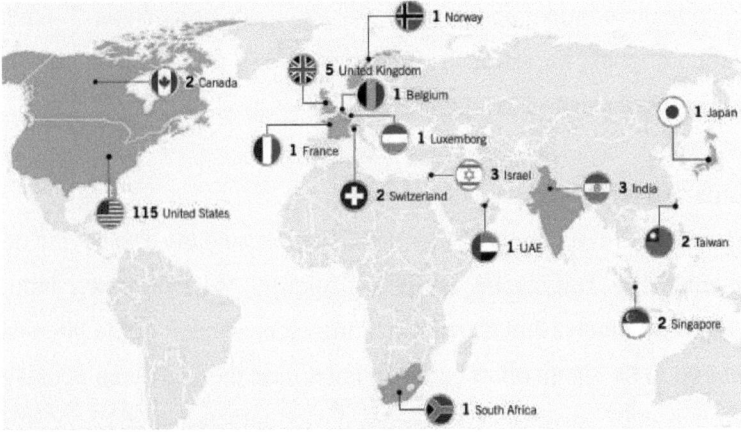

Figure 6. Observed Global APT1 Activity

Mandiant even cites the possible postal address of this unit and builds an estimate of its numbers and the infrastructure it uses. Mandiant suspects that the APT1 group has been operating since 2006 and that, over the past six years has managed to steal terabytes of data from at least 141 organizations. Most of the targeted companies are in English-speaking countries. [34]

3.4. TeamSpy

In March 2013 the Laboratory of Cryptography and System Security (Crysys) at Budapest University of Technology and Economics, released their research around a targeted attack they have identified, named TeamSpy.

This attack is cyber surveillance operation targeting high level political and human rights activists through CIS and Eastern Europe nations. Victims also include government agencies as well as private companies. The attacks have been ongoing for almost a decade and were previously mentioned by Belorussian activists in 2012.[35]

3.5. Stuxnet

In March 2013 Researchers at Symantec have traced the origins and design of Stuxnet, the first cyber weapon designed to shut down industrial facilities. It was found that Stuxnet 0.5, the older version of the virus widely considered to be a joint effort between Israel and the U.S., was actually first deployed in 2007, several years before it was detected in 2010. Moreover, its virus codes trace back to 2005. The importance of Stuxnet discovering was that this malware was followed by other dangerous cyber weapons. After Stuxnet was discovered, engineers found similar viruses with the names Duqu, Gauss, and Flame. The basis of Stuxnet malware code was similar with its followers. [36]

3.5. NetTraveler

A newly revealed global malware campaign hit 350 high-profile targets in 40 different countries. The cyberespionage campaign, codenamed Operation NetTraveler, has been active since at least 2004, stealing more than 22 gigabytes of data from computers around the world.

Figure 7. NetTraveler Attack

This campaign was discovered in June 2013. The malware attacks were uncovered by Russian online security company Kaspersky Lab. The hackers behind the campaign used a data-exfiltration tool called NetTraveler — not a very sophisticated malware designed to steal sensitive data and information.

The name originates from a string contained in the malware code: "NetTraveler is Running!"

Hackers used the malware, among others, to steal documents relating to space exploration, nanotechnologies, energy production, medicine and communications from government institutions, embassies, research centres, military contractors and energy industries. The researchers noted this was the same tool used to target Tibetan and Uyghur activists, two groups often targeted by Chinese hackers.

4. CYBER TERRORISM

The terrorists use cyberspace to cause uncertainty. They, for their own reasons, are struggling against state authorities and governments and use all available means to achieve their own aim. Cyber attacks occur in two forms, one used to attack data, and others focused on control systems. [37] Data theft and destruction leads to service sabotage and this is the most common form of Internet and computer attacks. The attacks focused on the control systems are used to disable or manipulate the physical infrastructure. For example, you can perform remote power supply networks, railway and water supplies in order to achieve a negative opinion on larger geographic areas. This is accomplished by sending data over the Internet or by penetrating security systems. These weak spots in the system were used in the incident in Australia that occurred in March 2000, where disgruntled employee (who failed to provide full-time employment) used the Internet to slip one million liters of unprocessed sewage into the river and coastal waters in Queensland. [37] In fact, after 44 unsuccessful tries, the 45th was successful. The first 44 trials were not detected at all.

After the September 11 attacks, the auditors of public safety are worried because the most critical infrastructures are owned by private companies, which are not always interested in possible security threats.

In 1988, a terrorist guerrilla organization, within two weeks, flood embassies of Sri Lanka with 800 email-s a day. The message which was appearing was "We are the Internet Black Tigers and we are doing this to disrupt your communications." Department of Intelligence characterizes the attack as the first known terrorist attack on government computer systems.

Internet saboteurs in 1998 attacked Web site of the Indian Bhabha Atomic Research Centre and stole e-mails from the same center. The three anonymous saboteurs through online interview claimed that they protest against recent nuclear explosions in India. [38] In July 1997, the leader of the Chinese hacker group claimed that temporarily disallowed Chinese satellite and announced that hackers set up a new global organization to protest and prevent investment by Western countries in China.

In September 1998, on the eve of parliamentary elections in Sweden, saboteurs attack the Web site of the right-wing political party in Sweden and created a link to a Web site on the left and to the pornographic sites. The same month, saboteurs attacked the website of the Mexican government in protest against government corruption and censorship. Analysts point out these crime examples as low level information warfare.

Romanian hackers on one occasion managed to intrude into the computer systems controlling the life support systems at an Antarctic research station, endangering the 58 scientists involved. Fortunately, their activity is stopped before any accident occurred.

During the Kosovo conflict, Belgrade hackers conducted a denial of service attack (DoS) on the NATO servers. They "flooded" NATO servers with ICMP Ping messages, typically used for diagnostic or control purposes or generated in response to errors in IP operations.

During the Palestinian-Israeli cyber war in 2000 similar attack has been used. Pro-Palestinian hackers used DoS tools to attack Israel's ISP (Internet Service Provider), Netvision. Although the attack was initially successful, Netvision managed to resist subsequent attacks by increasing its safety.

Also in April 2007, numerous journalistic organizations associated with the "Associated Press" reported that cyber attacks on critical information infrastructure on Estonia is conducted by computer servers located in Russia, although it was later determined that it is a Distributed DoS attacks carried out by different locations around the world (U.S., Canada, Brazil, Vietnam and other locations). Of course, the locations of the computers involved in the attack do not always shows the location of the direct participants in the attack. It is actually the location of the so-called "zombie" machines that act as intermediaries during the attack, without their knowledge or without any knowledge of the direct attackers. The attack completely put out the function of the Web sites of many governmental, media and financial institutions and leads to diplomatic talks which was a reason to examine the possibility of creating a NATO-supported research center capable of identifying the source of cyber attacks. In August 2008, a similar attack was conducted against Georgia. It is assumed that the attack was perpetrated by Russian hackers.

In October 2007, hackers attacked the Web site of Ukrainian President Viktor Jushenko. The responsibility for this attack took over the radical Russian nationalist youth group, the Eurasian Youth Movement.[1]

An analyst from the U.S. Central Intelligence Agency (CIA) publicly revealed that in January 2008, hackers successfully stopped power supply networks in several U.S. cities. In November 2008, the Pentagon had a problem with cyber attacks carried out by computer virus, prompting the Department of Defense (DoD) to take unprecedented step of banning the use of external hardware devices, such as flash memory devices and DVDs.[2] Officially, U.S. never felt cyber terrorist attack.

One of the examples that have caused global panic occurred in late 2008, when a group of hackers called "Greek Security Team", "intrude" into CERN computer systems (European Center for Nuclear Research) so deep, that they were very close to take control of one of the detectors at LHC (Large Hadron Collider), the largest particle accelerator. Hackers broke into the system on the first day of the experiment and placed a fake page on the site of CERN, whose aim was to defame the experts responsible for computer system, calling them "a group of students." CERN officials said that it was not caused any damage, but knowing that the detectors and all valuable equipment is vulnerable to digital threats is really uncomfortable.

4.1. Methods and techniques of the cyber terrorism

As we already explained, except for offensive operations the terrorist can

---

[1] Radio Free Europe, 2007
[2] FOX News, 2008

effectively use the cyberspace for secure communications. [39]

Information security is of great importance to many organizations, including the terrorists. The reason for this primarily lies in their malicious activities, so it is obvious that they will be faced with a well-equipped government security forces and coalition forces, that can easily reveal their intentions through the interception of communication using sophisticated monitoring equipment.

This problem is well known for the terrorist organizations, which is the reason for them to pay great attention to security aspects during the transmission of subtle information.

"Al Qaeda Training Manual" is just one of the many evidence of the commitment of terrorist organizations for safe communication. Notably, among the most important and most extensive lessons described in this guide are two lessons that provide guidance on the proper usage of communications and data protection. Special emphasis on this issue is placed in the thirteenth lesson "Secret Writing and Ciphers and Codes" which aim is to train potential members of this terrorist organization for secure data transmission.

Data hiding by the members of terrorist organizations is revealed on many occasions, but for sure it can be said that the number of cases where the data transmission covered using steganographic methods is not registered by security services is much larger.

Evidence for the use of steganography by al-Qaeda terrorist organization is the arrest in Berlin in 2012 of a 22 year old Austrian who had just arrived from Pakistan. Later it was confirmed that he is a member of this terrorist organization. The digital storage and memory cards he tried to hide were password protected and the information were invisible. After the initial analysis it was found that inside memory cards was buried a pornographic video "Kick Ass" and a file named "Sexy Tanja". A few weeks later, after great efforts to combat a password and the software to make the file almost invisible, German researchers encoded in the video of a treasure trove of intelligence – over 100 documents including al-Qaeda firsthand about some of the plots of the terrorist group and a bolder road map for future operations for which there were not specified neither the date nor the location. Also various terrorist training manuals used by this organization were found. All these data were hidden using steganographic tools.

The National Coordination Office (NCO) for Networking and Information Technology Research and Development (NITRD), in a report released in 2006's gave the following statement: [40]

- "......immediate concerns also include the use of cyberspace for covert communications, particularly by terrorists but also by foreign intelligence services; espionage against sensitive but poorly defended data in government and industry systems; subversion by insiders, including vendors and contractors; criminal activity, primarily involving fraud and theft of financial or identity information, by hackers and organized crime groups... "

- "International interest in R&D for Steganography technologies and their commercialization and application has exploded in recent years. These technologies pose a potential threat to national security. Because Steganography secretly embeds additional, and nearly undetectable, information content in digital products, the potential for covert dissemination of malicious software, mobile code, or information is great."

– "The threat posed by Steganography has been documented in numerous intelligence reports."

Rumors about the usage of Steganography by terrorists first appeared in the daily newspaper "USA Today", on 5 February 2001, in two articles titled as "Terrorist instructions hidden online" and "Terror groups hide behind Web encryption". In October 2001, the information looked even more precise: "militant wired Web links to jihad". In October 2001, "The New York Times" published an article claiming that al-Qaeda had used steganography techniques to encrypt and insert messages into images and then transported via e-mail and possibly via USENET to prepare and execute the September 11, 2001 terrorist attacks.

With reference to research on Jamestown Foundation, captured terrorist training manual "Technical Mujahid, a Training Manual for Jihadists", contains a section titled "Covert Communications and Hiding Secrets inside Images".

Centre for Steganographic Research and Analysis, during the latest research, identified more than 725 applications for digital steganography. [41]

5. NATIONAL RESPONSES TO THE CYBER TERRORISM THREAT

The European Commission adopted a provision that requires all members of the European Union all activities defined as "attack through interference with information systems" to be punishable as terrorist act, if their goal is "serious alteration or destruction of political, economic or social structures". France expanded police power to search private property without warrants. [42]

Spain, similar to the UK legislation, restricts the activities of any organization that is directly or indirectly related to the ETA (Euskadi Ta Askatasuna) - an armed separatist group for Basque Homeland and Freedom. The European Council took steps to establish the wanted level across Europe and to define the term "terrorist crime." Germany's government cuts the limits about monitoring telephone calls and monitoring e-mails and bank accounts and restores previously limited communication between the Secret Service and the police. In June 2002, the United Kingdom, under the pretext of counter-terrorism, tried to bring regulations that would mandate almost all local and national government agencies to gain access to data communications traffic without the need of a warrant. [43]

Australia introduced a law on terrorists in order to intercept electronic mail (giving power to the main Australian Security Intelligence Organisation), and to create an attack directed against the preparation and planning of terrorist acts. This law allows the terrorist property to be "frozen" or taken away. New Zealand has introduced similar legislation in order to comply with the bilateral agreement on legal harmonization between these two countries.

India also brought its own decree to protect against terrorism, enabling authorities to apprehend suspect without trial, to conduct surveillance and to seize money and property of suspected terrorists, and in some cases to implement the death penalty. [43]

Some states, such as is the case with the U.S. and Australia, recommended setting of network operation center in cyberspace, which will include Internet service providers, and developers (programmers) of computer hardware and software.

Their task is to develop safe technology, as intelligent analysis software, that will be able to analyze existing data, both public and private, in order to detect suspicious activities. [44]

6. MULTILATERAL RESPONSES TO THE THREATS OF CYBER TERRORISM

6.1. Response of cyber terrorism by the North Atlantic Treaty Organization (NATO)

As sophisticated political-military alliance, NATO has long been familiar with the use and defence of electronic and information warfare. For years, NATO is involved in efforts to transform the military organization and conduct of operations by "networking oriented warfare" and "network enabled capabilities". At the Prague Summit in November 2002, NATO leaders decided to strengthen its capabilities to defend against cyber attacks. Decision in Prague resulted in many initiatives. [45]

A new NATO Cyber Terrorism Program is initiated, involving various NATO bodies: NATO Communication and Information Systems Services Agency (NCSA), described as the "first line of defence against cyber terrorism," NATO INFOSEC Technical Centre (NITC), responsible for communication and computer security; NATO Information Assurance Operations Centre (NIAOC), responsible for management and coordination of cryptographic equipment in response to a cyber attack against NATO; NATO Computer Incident Response Capability (NCIRC), whose task is to protect the NATO encrypted communications systems.[46]

After the cyber attack against Estonia in April and May 2007, NATO ministers agreed on the outline of the NATO's cyber defence concept, which was brought in Nordwijk, in October 2008. [47] This concept at the beginning of 2008 was developed into a NATO Policy on Cyber Defence. [48] The NATO members were informed in more details about this policy on the NATO Summit held in Bucharest at the beginning of April 2008. [49]

Following the Summit, NATO established Cyber Defence Management Authority (CDMA), in order to bring together all key players in the NATO activities related to cyber defence, and better management of the cyber defence support to any member of the alliance in defence against cyber attack, upon request. [48] At the same time, NATO leaders agreed with the formal establishment of the NATO Cooperative Cyber Defence Center of Excellence (CCD-CoE), which has been in development since 2004. The significance of the CCD-CoE, based in Tallinn, was confirmed during the attack of Estonia in 2007, so in October 2008 the NATO Council grants the Centre full NATO accreditation and theorganisation obtains the status of International Military Organization. [50]

"The mission and vision" of the CCD-CoE are described as follows: "enhance the capability, cooperation and information sharing among NATO, NATO nations and partners in cyber defence by virtue of education, research and development, lessons learned and consultation" and to be "the main source of expertise in the field of cooperative cyber defence by accumulating, creating, and disseminating knowledge in related matters within NATO, NATO nations and partners". [51] The organization current has elevan "nations-sponsors": Estonia, Germany, Hungary, Italy, Latvia, Lithuania, the Netherlands, Poland, Slovakia, Spain and the USA. Invitation for membership is open to all NATO members, but cooperation projects are also conducted jointly with NATO partner countries, academia and the private sector.

6.2. United Nations (UN)

Cyber security is one of the main themes on the traditional debates on security policy in the UN system. Normally this refers to those debates related to the threat of terrorism and in the form of Resolutions of the UN Security Council. [52] The topic is covered in the work of the Counter Terrorism Committee established by Security Council, [53] and it is mentioned in the UN Global Counter-Terrorism Strategy.

In the latter case, the goal is not only "counter terrorism in all its forms and manifestations on the Internet", but also with more active approach to "use the Internet as a tool for countering the spread of terrorism."[54] Wider in the UN systems, cyber security is regularly recognized as a central feature that will be constantly developed in the international agenda for international security.

In the UN system, the International Telecommunication Union (ITU) has highest responsibility for the practical aspects and applications of the international cyber security.

The ITU mission statement embraces the issue of cyber security in direct terms. The purpose of the organization is to develop confidence in the use of cyberspace through enhanced online security. Achieving of the cyber security and cyber peace are some of the most critical concerns in the ICT development, and ITU takes concrete measures through its Global Cybersecurity Agenda (GCA). [55]

In September 2008, the ITU and the International Multilateral Partnership Against Cyber Threats (IMPACT) signed an agreement under which GCA is located in IMPACT headquarter in Cyberjaya, Malaysia.[56]

6.3. Organization for Economic Cooperation and Development (OECD)

Issued in 2002 by the Directorate for Science, Technology and Industry of the OECD, Guidelines for the Security of Information Systems and Networks have become a standard reference point for national and international cyber security initiatives. Non-binding guidelines adopted by 19 of the 30 members of the OECD as well as Brazil, and the European Union. The Guidelines apply to all participants in the new information society and suggest the need for a greater awareness and understanding of security issues and the need to develop a "culture of security".

The guidelines are based on nine complementary principles that organize and implement a safety culture: Awareness (the need for security of information systems and networks); Responsibility (all participants are responsible for the security of the information systems and networks); Response (participants should act on security incidents in timely and co-operative manner); Ethics (respect the legitimate interests of other users and promotion of best practice); Democracy (security measures should be compatible with the basic values of a democratic society); Risk assessment (broad assessment of threats and weaknesses as a basis for risk management); Security design and implementation (security measures should be an essential feature of information systems and networks); Security management (comprehensive approach involving all stakeholders at all levels, addressing threats as they appear); Reassessment (continuous review, revision and modification of security measures as risks evolve).[57]

Other cyber security initiatives include a series of OECD reports on information security and privacy, including topics such as national guidelines for information security, OECD guidelines for policies to identify radio frequency and many others, [58] and finally the Working Party on Security of Information and Privacy (WPSIP), which aims is to provide a "foundation for developing national coordinated policies." [59]

6.4. Organization for Security and Co-operation in Europe (OSCE)

OSCE's interest in the challenges of cyber security is increasing. In December 2004, the OSCE Ministerial Council decided to dedicate to the "extent of use of the Internet by terrorist organizations", including a number of activities, such as recruiting of the terrorists, foundation, organization and propaganda. [60] Two years later, the foreign ministers called for greater international cooperation and utilizing more effort to protect "vital critical information infrastructures and networks from the threat of cyber attacks."

The participating countries were asked to closely monitor Web pages of the terrorist and extremist organizations and to exchange information with other governments in the OSCE and other relevant forums and it is asked "more active participation of civil society institutions and the private sector in preventing and countering the use of the Internet for terrorist purposes."[61] OSCE's Permanent Council has also been a venue for debate and discussion concerning cyber security. [62] In June 2008, for example, Estonian Defence Minister Jaak Aaviksoo spoke about immense amount of work that has to be done in the the field of cyber security. [63]

The OSCE's Forum for Security Co-operation (FSC) also contributed to the organization's involvement in the field of cyber security. Although the FSC's work has been concentrated largely on arms control, disarmament and confidence-building measures, [64] lately, the forum began to be more interested in cyber security. In October 2008, FBS (in joint session with the Permanent Council) decided to convene an OSCE workshop on a Comprehensive approach to improving cyber security in March 2009. [65] Finally, the OSCE supports national efforts, such as the Armenian Forces on Cyber Crime and Cyber Security. [66]

6.5. Council of Europe (CoE)

Contribution of the CoE in the international cyber security policy is primarily through the Convention on Cyber Crime, which was opened for signature in November 2001 and which entered into force in July 2004. It is important to note that, although the Convention was signed by 46 countries, including Canada, Japan, South Africa and the U.S., until today it has been ratified by only 26 countries, including Macedonia, Albania, Croatia, Estonia, Hungary, Lithuania, Romania and Slovenia, 11EU states have yet to ratified the Convention and five CoE member states have not even signed (including Russia). Convention was signed and ratified by countries that are not members of the CoE (Canada, Japan, South Africa and USA).[67, 68, 69] Sixteen other countries that are not members of the Council of Europe are reported as "known to use the Convention as a guideline for their national legislation" (including Brazil and India).

The CoE Convention on Cybercrime is important for several aspects. First, the Convention addresses the illegal activities and practices that features across spectrum of cyber security threats. Second, the Convention establishes common standards and procedures that are legally binding on its signatories. Third, the Convention is open to the Member States of the CoE and others, which increases its authority as an international instrument.

Finally, the Convention introduced requirements for handling data and access that have led to concerns about the privacy law and civil liberties.

6.6. G-8

The main contribution of the G-8 in international cyber security policy is a Subgroup of High-Tech Crime, created as a subset of Lyon Group in 1996 to combat transnational organized crime. [70]The purpose of this subgroup was to "enhance the ability of the G-8 countries to protect, investigate and prosecute crimes committed using computers, network communications, and other new technologies." The mission of the subunit was subsequently extended to include the use of the Internet by terrorists and the protection of critical information infrastructure. Subgroup is trying to deal with cyber crime not only within the jurisdiction of the G8 countries, but also to create guidelines that could take and implement other countries. The subgroup has created 24/7 network of contact for high-tech crime and international Critical Information Infrastructure Protection (CCIP) Directory. Subgroup has published its best practice documents and guidelines for assessment of threats to computer and network security and has organized international training conferences for cyber-crime agencies.

7. DOES INTERNATIONAL HUMANITARIAN LOW APPLY TO CYBER ATTACK AND CYBER TERRORISM?

Information and communications networks are largely owned and operated by the private sector, both nationally and internationally. Thus, addressing network security issues requires a public-private partnership as well as international cooperation and norms. [71]

The international cyber incidents witnessed by the international community in the past decade have awaked the international discussion on the regulation of the domain that is developing into a self-standing dimension of our daily life, national security and warfare.

Regarded cyberspace as one of the great "commons", the purpose of taking this perspective is to evaluate the usefulness of the commons regulation analogy for resolving some of the issues nations and international community faces in regard to cyber security, and for guiding the development of a regulatory framework for cyberspace.

The actual question nowadays is: Is there a legal vacuum in cyber space? Cordula Droege, an ICRC legal expert, explains that the existing legal framework is applicable and must be respected even in the cyber realm. [72]

International humanitarian law (IHL) only comes into play if cyber operations are committed in the context of an armed conflict – whether between states, between states and organized armed groups or between organized armed groups. Therefore, we need to distinguish the general issue of cyber security from the specific issue of cyber operations in armed conflict. Terms like "cyber attacks" or even "cyber terrorism" may evoke methods of warfare, but the operations they refer to are not necessarily conducted in armed conflict.

But, IHL does not specifically mention cyber operations. Because of this, and because the exploitation of cyber technology is relatively new and sometimes appears to introduce a complete qualitative change in the means and methods of warfare, it has occasionally been argued that IHL is unwell adapted to the cyber realm and cannot be applied to cyber warfare.

New technologies of all kinds are being developed all the time and IHL is sufficiently broad to accommodate these developments. This is not to say that there might not be a need to develop the law further as technologies evolve or their humanitarian impact becomes better understood. That will have to be determined by States. In the meantime, it is important to stress that there is no legal vacuum in cyber space. [72] Beyond that, however, we are faced with a number of question marks on how IHL will apply in practice.

It is unconscionable that cyber crime is going unpunished to the degree that it is around the world. Technology alone is not the answer. The governments must adopt stronger cyber crime legislation in order to have a rule to protect and serve in the digital world. Greater international cooperation and uniformity in laws and punishment is needed in order to counter today's most sophisticated cyber crime threats such as the widespread use of underground economy servers. [73]

8. CONCLUSION

This book gives a short overview of the terms of cyber attacks and cyber terrorism and describes the most known cyber attacks and cyber terrorist attacks. Taking in consideration the fact that the cyber terrorists are using smarter methods and tools to attack computer systems and government institutions, and the main objective is to achieve their objectives; the national and global security are subject to higher risk.

The part of the book represents a response to the cyber security challenges at national level and by various international organizations. NATO, for example, is a long-standing political and military organization, with extensive experience in the field of cyber terrorism and cyber security.

One of the limitations that occur during the acquisition of various cyber security measures is a balance to be made between security measures and civil liberties. There should be also a balance between the provision of specific interests to a particular organization or government, and more general requirements for the benefit of all legitimate users to be formed an international communications and technological environment that will be unfriendly-oriented to the ambitions of cyber terrorists and extremists, cyber criminals and hackers.

REFERENCES

[1]   S. Best, *Defining Terrorism*:
      http://www.drstevebest.org/Essays/Defining%20Terrorism.htm   Last
      accessed 21.12.2013

[2]   Sarah Gordon and Richard Ford, Cyberterrorism, Symantec, 2003,
      www.symantec.com/avcenter/reference/cyberterrorism.pdf   Last
      accessed 21.12.2013

[3]   M. Cereijo Cuba the threat II: Cyberterrorism and Cyberwar, 16 Maj
      2006:   http://www.lanuevacuba.com/archivo/manuel-cereijo-110.htm
      Last accessed 21.12.2013

[4]   R. L. Dick, Director, National Infrastructure Protection Center, FBI
      Federal Bureau of Investigation, *Before the House Energy and
      Commerce Committee, Oversight and Investigation Subcomittee
      Washington*, DC, 05 April 2001,
      http://www.fbi.gov/news/testimony/issue-of-intrusions-into-government-
      computer-networks Last accessed 21.12.2013

[5]   *www.terror.net: How Modern Terrorism Uses the Internet*, 21 February
      2007:   http://www.asiantribune.com/index.php?q=node/4627   Last
      accessed 21.12.2013

[6] M.Bogdanoski, D. Petreski, Cyber Terrorism–Global Security Threat, *Contemporary Macedonian Defense-International Scientific Defense, Security and Peace Journal*, 13(24), 59-73.

[7] "GCHQ chief reports 'disturbing' cyber-attacks on UK", BBC news UK, 31.10.2011, http://www.bbc.co.uk/news/uk-15516959, Last accessed 21.12.2013

[8] E. Kain, "Cyber attacks take down two Israeli websites - is cyber warfare the next front in the middle east conflict?", FORBES, 16.01.2012, http://www.forbes.com/sites/erikkain/2012/01/16/cyber-attacks-take-down-two-israeli-websites-is-cyber-warfare-the-next-front-in-the-middle-east-conflict/, Last accessed 21.12.2013

[9] B. Acohido, Cyberattacks likely to escalate this year, US Today, 10.01.2012, http://usatoday30.usatoday.com/tech/news/story/2012-01-08/hacktivism-lulzsec-anonymous/52489606/1, Last accessed 21.12.2013

[10] Cyber-attacks now the most feared EU energy threat, Euractive, 25.01.2011, http://www.euractiv.com/energy/cyber-attacks-feared-eu-energy-threat-news-501547, Last accessed 21.12.2013

[11] J. P Mello Jr, Cyberattacks the greatest threat to nations, say global execsm, CSO, 13.06.2013, http://www.csoonline.com/article/735485/cyberattacks-the-greatest-threat-to-nations-say-global-execs, Last accessed 21.12.2013

[12] 2012 Cost of Cyber Crime Study: United States 2012, Ponemon Institute, October 2012, http://www.ponemon.org/local/upload/file/2012_US_Cost_of_Cyber_Crime_Study_FINAL6%20.pdf, Last accessed 21.12.2013

[13] J. Kirk, Deep cyberattacks cause millions in losses for U.S. banks, Computerworld, 22.09.2013, http://www.computerworld.com/s/article/9241852/Deep_cyberattacks_cause_millions_in_losses_for_U.S._banks, Last accessed 21.12.2013

[14] "Strategic Concept For the Defence and Security of The Members of the North Atlantic TreatyOrganisation", Adopted by Heads of State and Government in Lisbon, November 2010, http://www.nato.int/lisbon2010/strategic-concept-2010-eng.pdf, Last accessed 21.12.2013

[15] "A Strong Britain in an Age of Uncertainty: The National Security Strategy, United Kingdom", October 2010,http://www.direct.gov.uk/prod_consum_dg/groups/dg_digitalassets/@dg/@en/documents/digitalasset/dg_191639.pdf, Last accessed 21.12.2013

[16] "National Security Strategy, Unite States of America", May 2010, http://www.whitehouse.gov/sites/default/files/rss_viewer/national_security_strategy.pdf, Last accessed 21.12.2013

[17] "International Strategy For Cyberpace, Prosperity, Security, and Openness in a Networked World", President of the United States, May 2011,http://info.publicintelligence.net/WH-InternationalCyberspace.pdf, Last accessed 21.12.2013

[18] H. Mirza, "Cyber-Attacks Are the Biggest National Security Threat", Policymic, August 2011, http://www.policymic.com/articles/1518/cyber-attacks-are-the-biggest-national-security-threat, Last accessed 21.12.2013

[19] S. Pelley, Panetta: Cyber warfare could paralyze U.S., CBS News, 05.01.2012,

http://www.cbsnews.com/8301-18563_162-57353420/panetta-cyber-warfare-could-paralyze-u.s/, Last accessed 21.12.2013

[20] R.C. Hodgin, "FBI ranks cyber attacks third most dangerous behind nuclear war and WMDs", TD Daily, 7 January 2009, http://www.tgdaily.com/security-features/40861-fbi-ranks-cyber-attacks-third-most-dangerous-behind-nuclear-war-and-wmds, Last accessed 21.12.2013

[21] "Investigating Cyber Security Threats: Exploring National Security and Law Enforcement Perspectives", Frederic Lemieux, Report GW-CSPRI-2011-2, 7 April 2011, http://www.cspri.seas.gwu.edu/uploads/2/1/3/2/21324690/2011-2_investigating_cyber_security_threats_lemieux.pdf, Last accessed 21.12.2013

[22] Worst Cyber Attack on U.S. Military Came Via Flash Drive: U.S., DefenceNews, 25.09.2010, http://www.defensenews.com/article/20100825/DEFSECT04/8250303/Worst-Cyber-Attack-U-S-Military-Came-Via-Flash-Drive-U-S-, Last accessed 21.12.2013

[23] M. Bogdanoski, A. Risteski, M. Bogdanoski, Industrial Cyber Attacks – Global Security Threat, March 2012; In proceeding of: International conference "The Faces of the Crisis"

[24] Cyberattack against Telenor, The Norway Post, 26.05.2013, http://www.norwaypost.no/index.php/business/general-business/28565-cyberattack-against-telenor-, Last accessed 21.12.2013

[25] Hacking Attack Hits ITU Website During Ongoing Meet In Dubai, CBR, 07.12.2012, http://www.cbronline.com/news/security/hacking-attack-

hits-itu-website-during-ongoing-meet-in-dubai-071212, Last accessed 21.12.2013

[26] H. T. Klaar, "Cyber Security Threats and Responses at Global, Nation-State, Industry and Individual Levels", 2011, http://www.sciencespo.fr/ceri/sites/sciencespo.fr.ceri/files/art_htk.pdf, Last accessed 21.12.2013

[27] T. Rains, Using the Past to Predict the Future: Top 5 Threat Predictions for 2013, Microsoft Security Blog, 13.12.2012, http://blogs.technet.com/b/security/archive/2012/12/13/using-the-past-to-predict-the-future-top-5-threat-predictions-for-2013.aspx, Last accessed 21.12.2013

[28] 2013 Threats Predictions, McAfee Labs, 2012, http://www.mcafee.com/us/resources/reports/rp-threat-predictions-2013.pdf, Last accessed 21.12.2013

[29] D. Banning, J. Hainaut, Top Cyber Threats: Making Sense of All the 2013 Predictions, Experis Manpower Group, March 2013, http://www.experis.us/Website-File-Pile/Webinar-Recordings/Experis/Presentation-Materials/Cyber-Threats-Presentation-Material, Last accessed 21.12.2013

[30] P. Passeri, July 2013 Cyber Attacks Statistics, Hackmageddon, August 2013,http://hackmageddon.com/2013/09/07/august-2013-cyber-attacks-statistics/, Last accessed 15.09.2013

[31] M. Bogdanoski, T. Shuminoski, A. Risteski, Analysis of the SYN Flood DoS Attack, *International Journal of Computer Network and Information Security (IJCNIS)*, 5(8), 1, 2013

[32] Kaspersky Lab Identifies Operation "Red October," an Advanced Cyber-Espionage Campaign Targeting Diplomatic and Government Institutions

Worldwide, Kasperky Lab, January 2013, http://www.kaspersky.com/about/news/virus/2013/Kaspersky_Lab_Ide ntifies_Operation_Red_October_an_Advanced_Cyber_Espionage_Ca mpaign_Targeting_Diplomatic_and_Government_Institutions_Worldwi de, Last accessed 21.12.2013

[33] Kaspersky Lab Identifies 'MiniDuke', a New Malicious Program Designed for Spying on Multiple Government Entities and Institutions Across the World, Kastersky Lab, February 2013, http://www.kaspersky.com/about/news/virus/2013/Kaspersky_Lab_Ide ntifies_MiniDuke_a_New_Malicious_Program_Designed_for_Spying_o n_Multiple_Government_Entities_and_Institutions_Across_the_World, Last accessed 21.12.2013

[34] APT1: Exposing One of China's Cyber Espionage Units, Mandiant, February 2013, http://intelreport.mandiant.com/Mandiant_APT1_Report.pdf, Last accessed 21.12.2013

[35] TeamSpy – Obshie manevri. Ispolzovat' tolko s razreshenija S-a. v1, Laboratory of Cryptography and System Security (CrySyS Lab), Technical Report, March 2013, http://www.crysys.hu/teamspy/teamspy.pdf, Last accessed 21.12.2013

[36] G. McDonald, L. O Murchu, S. Doherty, R. Chien, Stuxnet 0.5: The Missing Link, Symantec, February 2013, http://www2.gwu.edu/~nsarchiv/NSAEBB/NSAEBB424/docs/Cyber-088.pdf, Last accessed 21.12.2013

[37] R. Lemos, *Cyberterrorism: The real risk*, 2002: http://www.crime-research.org/library/Robert1.htm Last accessed 21.12.2013

[38] D.Briere, P.Hurley, *Wireless network hacks and mods for dummies*, 2005, Wiley.

[39] M. Bogdanoski, A. Risteski, & S. Pejoski, (2012, November). *Steganalysis—A way forward against cyber terrorism*. In Telecommunications Forum (TELFOR), 2012 20th (pp. 681-684). IEEE.

[40] A. Jahangiri, *Cyberspace, Cyberterrorism and Information Warfare: A Perfect Recipe for Confusion:* http://www.alijahangiri.org/publication/Cyberspace-Cyberterrorism-and-Information-Warfare-A-Perfect-Recipe-for-Confusion.htm

[41] E. S. Othman, *Hide and Seek: Embedding Audio into RGB 24-bit Color Image Sporadically Using Linked List Concepts:* IOSR Journal of Computer Engineering (IOSRJCE), Volume 4, Issue 1 (Sep-Oct. 2012), PP 37-44, http://iosrjournals.org/iosr-jce/papers/Vol4-issue1/G0413744.pdf Last accessed 21.12.2013

[42] E. Waak, *The Global Reach of Privacy Invasion*, Humanist, November/December 2002 http://www.thehumanist.org/humanist/articles/waakND02.htm

[43] K. Curran&Others, *Civil Liberties and Computer Monitoring*, 2004: http://www.jiti.com/v05/jiti.v5n1.029-038.pdf Last accessed 21.12.2013

[44] B. Simons, , & E. H. Spafford, Inside Risks 153 , *Communications of the ACM, 46*(3), March 2003

[45] NATO Prague Summit Declaration Article 4(f), 21 November 2002: http://www.nato.int/docu/pr/2002/p02-127e.htm. Last accessed 21.12.2013

[46] NATO Communication and Information Systems Services Agency: http://www.ncsa.nato.int/topics/combating_cyber_terrorism.htm Last accessed 21.12.2013

[47] European Security and Defence Assembly, *Cyber warfare* (Assembly of the Western European Union, Defence Committee Report C/2022.), 5 November 2008

[48] NATO, *Defence against cyber attacks*, 26 June 2008: http://www.nato.int/issues/cyber_defence/index.html. Last accessed 21.12.2013

[49] NATO, *Bucharest Summit Declaration*, Art. 47, 3 April 2008: http://www.nato.int/docu/pr/2008/p08-049e.html. Last accessed 21.12.2013

[50] NATO, *Defending against cyber attacks: what does this mean in practice?*, 31 March 2008: http://www.nato.int/issues/cyber_defence/practice.html. Last accessed 21.12.2013

[51] CCD-CoE, *History and way ahead*: http://www.ccdcoe.org/12.html Last accessed 21.12.2013

[52] CCD-CoE, *Mission and Vision:* http://www.ccdcoe.org/11.html Last accessed 21.12.2013

[53] UN General Assembly, *The United Nations Global Counter-Terrorism Strategy* (A/Res/60/288, 20 September 2006), paras 12(a), 12(b): http://daccessdds.un.org/doc/UNDOC/GEN/N05/504/88/PDF/N0550488.pdf?OpenElement. Last accessed 21.12.2013

[54] The Use of Interent for Terrorist Purposed: United Nations Office on Drugs and Crime - Viena, (September 2012, p.vi),

http://www.unodc.org/documents/frontpage/Use_of_Internet_for_Terro rist_Purposes.pdf. Last accessed 21.12.2013

[55] ITU Global Cybersecurity Agenda (GCA, Framework for International Cooperation in Cybersecurity), ITU 2007, http://www.ifap.ru/library/book169.pdf Last accessed 21.12.2013

[56] Curbing Cyberthreats – IMPACT: http://www.itu.int/osg/csd/cybersecurity/gca/impact/index.html Last accessed 21.12.2013

[57] OECD, *Guidelines for the Security of Information Systems and Networks: Toward a Culture of Security* (Paris: OECD, 25 July, 2002): http://www.oecd.org/document/42/0,3343,en_2649_34255_15582250_1_1_1_1,00.html Last accessed 21.12.2013

[58] OECD Resources on Policy Issues Related to Internet Governance: http://www.oecd.org/document/21/0,3343,en_21571361_34590630_34591253_1_1_1_1,00.html Last accessed 21.12.2013

[59] OECD Working Part on Information Security and Privacy: http://www.oecd.org/document/46/0,3343,en_2649_34255_36862382_1_1_1_1,00.html, Last accessed 21.12.2013

[60] OSCE Ministerial Council Decision 3/04: *Combating the Use of the Internet for Terrorist Purposes*, 7 December 2004: http://www.osce.org/documents/mcs/2004/12/3906_en.pdf Last accessed 21.12.2013

[61] OSCE Ministerial Council Decision 7/06: *Countering the Use of the Internet for Terrorist Purposes*, 5 December 2006: http://www.osce.org/documents/mcs/2006/12/22559_en.pdf Last accessed 21.12.2013

[62] OSCE Permanent Council: http://www.osce.org/pc/

[63] OSCE Permanent Council, *OSCE can play important role in cyber security, says Estonian defence Minister*, Vienna, 4 June 2008: http://www.osce.org/pc/item_1_31483.htm Last accessed 21.12.2013

[64] OSCE Forum for Security Co-operation: http://www.osce.org/fsc/ Last accessed 21.12.2013

[65] OSCE FSC/PC 36th Joint Meeting, FSC Decision No. 10/08, *OSCE Workshop on a Comprehensive OSCE Approach to Enhancing Cyber Security*, 29th October 2008: http://www.osce.org/fsc/ Last accessed 21.12.2013

[66] OSCE, *OSCE office organises discussion in Yerevan on cyber security threats*, 21 March 2006: http://www.osce.org/item/18450.html Last accessed 21.12.2013

[67] Council of Europe Convention on Cybercrime: http://www.i-policy.org/2010/06/council-of-europe-convention-on-cybercrime.html Last accessed 21.12.2013

[68] Council of Europe Convention on Cybercrime: http://conventions.coe.int/treaty/Commun/ChercheSig.asp?NT=185&CM=8&DF=&CL=ENG Last accessed 21.12.2013

[69] Council of Europe, *Global reach of the Council of Europe Convention on Cybercrime*: http://www.coe.int/t/dc/files/themes/cybercrime/WorldMapCybercrime_E_2008_10_06.pdf Last accessed 21.12.2013

[70] Amandine Scherrer, G8 against Transnational Organized Crime (Global Finance), Ashgate Publishing Limited, 2009

[71] Radica Gareva, International community must focus on effective coordinated measures that will mitigate critical information infrastructure

cyber security challenges, scientific-professional military conference MILCON'12, Skopje, R. Macedonia, 14.05.2012

[72] Cordula Droege, No legal vacuum in cyber space, International Committee of the Red Cross, http://www.icrc.org/eng/resources/documents/interview/2011/cyber-warfare-interview-2011-08-16.htm Last accessed 21.12.2013

[73] John Thompson, "The Fight for Cyber Space: High Tech and Law Enforcement Experts on Defeating Today's Cyber Criminals, BSA 2007, http://www.bsa.org/policy Last accessed 21.12.2013

Printed by Books on Demand GmbH, Norderstedt / Germany